D1305331

ROCKCRAWLING

RACE CAR LEGENDS

COLLECTOR'S EDITION

Jeff Burton

Dale Earnhardt Jr.

Famous Finishes

Famous Tracks

Kenny Irwin Jr.

Jimmie Johnson

The Labonte Brothers

Lowriders

Monster Trucks & Tractors

Motorcycles

Off-Road Racing

Rockcrawling

Tony Stewart

The Unsers

Rusty Wallace

ROCKCRAWLING

Sue Mead

CHELSEA HOUSE PUBLISHERS

Cover Photo: A competitor in a Super Modified class rig climbs up a 25-foot cliff at a rockcrawling event held in Jellico, Tennessee.

CHELSEA HOUSE PUBLISHERS

VP, NEW PRODUCT DEVELOPMENT   Sally Cheney
DIRECTOR OF PRODUCTION   Kim Shinners
CREATIVE MANAGER   Takeshi Takahashi
MANUFACTURING MANAGER   Diann Grasse

STAFF FOR ROCKCRAWLING

EDITORIAL ASSISTANT Sarah Sharpless
PRODUCTION EDITOR Bonnie Cohen
PHOTO EDITOR Pat Holl
SERIES DESIGN AND LAYOUT Hierophant Publishing Services/EON PreMedia

http://www.chelseahouse.com

First Printing

1   3   5   7   9   8   6   4   2

Library of Congress Cataloging-in-Publication Data

Mead, Sue.
   Rockcrawling / Sue Mead.
      p. cm.—(Race car legends. Collector's edition)
   Includes bibliographical references and index.
   ISBN 0-7910-8691-7
   1. Rockcrawling.   I. Title. II. Series.
GV1029.R63M43 2005
796.7—dc22
                                                        2005010416

TABLE OF CONTENTS

1

HOW IT ALL BEGAN

Rockcrawling has been around for many years in the form of a recreational activity and as a category of four-wheeling. In different parts of the country, four-wheeling trails include terrains of dirt, mud, rocks or boulders, water crossings, and hill climbs. For many off-roaders, the mix of conditions is what's fun and makes off-pavement driving unique. But some develop a preference to a particular type of four-wheeling, such as crawling up and over rocks. To do this, they modify their vehicles for that terrain by adding bigger or stronger parts. As important as having your vehicle set up with the right equipment, you must become a skilled driver to navigate this tougher or more technical terrain. In the case of four-wheeling, competition leads to seeing who has the best vehicle for the terrain and who is the most talented driver or has the top driving team. You'll learn these almost always go hand in hand.

Such is the case with rockcrawling. How Ranch Pratt changed rockcrawling from a recreational sport to a formal, organized, and competitive sport will go down in history. People watch this sport at outdoor events (up-close and personal on the rocks), indoor events (shows with hand-built or fabricated courses), and in televised events.

These off-roaders enjoy climbing over rocks during their four-wheeling adventures. Rockcrawling has developed into a competitive motorsport with rules and a points system for scoring.

Ranch Pratt grew up in Salt Lake City, Utah, where the red rock of Wasatch Mountains is the backdrop to the sky. Though he loved the outdoors,[1] he didn't go four-wheeling until he was 22 years old. His father-in-law, Dave White, loved to go to **Moab**, Utah, and convinced Ranch to go along for a ride. That changed Ranch's life!

Moab is located in the heart of the Colorado Plateau and is called a national treasure and a geological wonder in guide books. Hundreds of thousands of 4WD (Four wheel drive) enthusiasts know it as the site for some of the best and most

The Colorado Plateau, a spectacular natural wonder, draws thousands of 4WD enthusiasts who drive on the rocks and trails that are carved out of the cliffs.

varied four- wheeling in the country. There are thousands of miles of backcountry trails, most of them from mining days.

Here, enthusiasts can explore the mixed terrain of deserts and canyons and motor on trails that range from a difficulty of #1 (Not Technical: Unimproved or rarely graded roads, 4WD or extra under carriage clearance needed at times, with no special driving skill required) to a #5 (Most Technical: Locking differentials and tow hooks, front and rear, necessary. Winch urgently recommended-unless you travel with someone who has one and can pull you out. Expert driving skill is critical.) This is the rating system for Moab, a scale of one to five, while other locations, such as the Rubicon Trail, are rated on a system of one to ten, with ten as the most difficult or technical trail.

What most people come to Moab to do, however, is drive on the rocks and the trails that are carved on cliff edges or enormous rock slabs. Ranch and Dave went to Moab in a stock, or straight-from-the-factory, Toyota pickup truck. That meant they could only drive on the non-technical trails. But, Ranch had his eyes open wide, and when he saw a Jeep Wrangler CJ, that had been set up for more **technical driving**, (it was "lifted and had lockers"[2]), he was hooked. "It blew me away how this Jeep could crawl over everything," he said. "I went back home and quit my job at an archery manufacturing company, and went to work for MEPCO (Military Equipment Parts Company)."[3] This gave Ranch the opportunity to learn more about "parts"[4] and how to design and build them for different types of vehicles.

In 1996, when Jeep came out with a new generation Wrangler, called the TJ, Ranch and Mark Falkner decided to take a TJ and add some heavy-duty parts to it. Mark's father had started MEPCO in 1959, and Ranch credits Mark with "great engineering talent and knowing how things work."[5] The pair started their own company, called Terraflex. They began to design heavy-duty parts for vehicles to help them travel over rough terrain, especially for rockcrawling. This meant Ranch spent a lot of time driving on rocks and meeting others with this passion.

In 1999, Ranch began the first rockcrawling series and formed the **American Rockcrawlers Association (ARCA)**. The first event was held in Farmington, New Mexico. "At that event, the goal of the sport was well on its way. ARCA started with a structured rule system, mainstream advertising, event programs and major corporate backing. It should be noted that the sport was also driven by the foresight of Goodyear Tire & Rubber Company, and there were many who believed in the concept and are also responsible for its growth," said Ranch.[6]

Some of the other fundamental players and the role they played in this sport's early development were Robert Don Pratt (Course Marshal), Phillip Collard (Course Designer), Sandee McCullen (Land Use Coordinator), Erica J. Pratt (Scoring), Gary and Becky Turpstra (Judges), Dave and George White (Marshals).

In 2001, the name was changed to the Rockcrawlers Association of America (RCAA). This gave room for the previous acronym to be used for the American Race Car Association, an organization that had been around for sometime.

DID YOU KNOW?

Though rockcrawling still pales in comparison to the interest and support of off-road races, such as the Baja 1000 and the Paris Dakar rally, its popularity increases each year. Rockcrawling vehicles are unique machines that look like a mix of an automobile, truck, and bug. They take drivers to the tops of cliffs and rock faces without the use of any road, dirt, paved, or otherwise.

Rockcrawling may sound like a foreign concept to many. Is it related to rock climbing, which uses harnesses and human strength to climb mountains? Is it an offshoot of off-roading, in which drivers use special techniques to achieve glory? Well, it's a little bit of both and a lot of fun.

The next development took place in 2002, when the Utah Rockcrawling & Off-Road Challenge was formed by Craig Stumph and aided by the RCAA. The idea was to build stronger "grassroots" support.[7] Soon, other partners were brought in for financial and marketing support to the Utah organization as the sport was quickly growing and gaining a larger following. Late in 2003, Stumph was bought out by Mark and Mike Patey, and Jeff Knowles, who also approached Ranch and the RCAA for a merger. A new entity, known as **United Rockcrawling & Off-Road Challenge (UROC)** was formed. Ranch is the CEO, Mark Patey is President, and Mike Patey and Jeff Knowles are silent partners.

Ranch Pratt, shown above, organized the first rockcrawling association and competitive events.

Today, Ranch spends all of his time with Terraflex, UROC, and a marketing company called Stonegate Media. Among this entrepreneur's many talents is the ability to build manmade or fabricated rockcrawling courses for competitions or demonstrations in cities, along with other commercial and industry trade shows.

"They say never make a business out of your hobby," said Ranch, "but my Mom always said do what you love and the money will come. I still love to go four-wheeling, to hear tires 'barking' on the rocks (this happens when the rubber makes noise skipping and sliding along rock surfaces). It hits all of your senses, especially the beauty you see when you go four-wheeling. When I go four-wheeling, I feel like I'm on

This off-road vehicle is designed to be able to ascend a steep mountainside. Heavy-duty parts and oversized wheels are often added on to help vehicles travel over rough terrain.

vacation, even though I'm working."[8] And it all started with one trip to Moab. A passion, a career, and a newly organized competitive sport were born.

② THE PLAYERS

Though rockcrawling is officially a young sport, many competitors got their starts long before Ranch Pratt's first event. Off-road racing great Walker Evans, for example, began competing in off-road vehicles decades ago. "I did off-road racing for 31 years," says Evans. "I started in desert racing, with the Baja 1000 being one of my main events. At first, I always ran a 2WD pickup, but in that last five years of desert racing, I got into trophy trucks. Altogether, I won the Baja 1000 nine times."[9] The first of Evans's Baja 1000 victories occurred in 1970 and the last in 1986.

Another major victory for Evans came in 1999, when he won the Championship Off-Road Racing (CORR) Pro-4 Points Championship. After that win, Evans retired, deciding to "step out of the sport on top."[10] But Goodyear, one of Evans's main sponsors, had a different idea. It wanted Evans to keep competing off-road. Therefore, Goodyear proposed that Evans begin competing in rockcrawling events. Immediately, Evans appreciated the new sport for its laid-back approach. "Crawling is not as strenuous as desert racing, and you don't need such a big crew. When you run Baja, you need 18 to 30 people by your side. With rockcrawling, you can load your **rig** on a flatbed trailer,

Walker Evans stands next to his truck. After retiring from an off-road racing career that spanned more than 30 years, Evans began competing in rockcrawling events.

and head out with a couple other guys. You'll have a heck of a time."[11]

When asked if he'll ever return to Baja racing, Evans, now in his late sixties, replied, "No, I did it for 31 years and now I'm done. Rockcrawling is good for me right now."[12] But that doesn't mean he's lost any of his competitive edge. Regarding the upcoming season, Evans' goal is simple and direct. "My plan is to win the championship in the UROC Unlimited class," he points out. "When I compete, I'm in it to win."[13]

Not everyone enters the sport of rockcrawling with nine Baja 1000 victories under his or her belt. But many of today's best competitors have backgrounds in off-road racing that extend back to the days before the sport was sanctioned.

Walker Evans is shown racing through the desert. Evans, who won the Baja 1000 nine times, now enjoys the more laid back approach in rockcrawling competitions.

Take Jeff Mello, a 37-year-old crawler from the Bay area in California. Mello's history includes mud dragging, sand racing, barrel racing, and Pro Stadium truck driving. He's also been a member of the Contra Costa Jeepers for life. But for Jeff, his interest in off-road sports started long before any official events took place. "I've been into four-wheeling since I was in the womb," says Mello. "So has my three-year-old daughter, Courtney, and my son, on the way, will be as well."[14]

"Rockcrawling became 'professional' back in 1998, when people began competing for real money," explains Mello. "Many crawlers, however, had been practicing the sport for years before, but it was all about trail enjoyment back then. This recreational riding took place in the sand, snow, and mud. I live in the Bay area, so the Rubicon Trail is

Jeff Mello is surrounded by the awards won in his 1979 Jeep CJ-7, an example of a rockcrawler in the Stock Modified class. There are currently 12–16 competitions per year held at various courses located throughout the country.

about three and a half hours away. Since that trail is mostly rock, someone along the line coined driving over it, 'rock-crawling.'"[15]

Mello competes in the Stock Modified class, which means he runs a street-legal Jeep on 35-inch tires. He's currently building a modified Jeep, which will still resemble a vehicle you would see on the road. That is, the engine is in the front, the front axle steers, the rear axle doesn't steer, and there are two seats next to each other. Mello recognizes that more capable vehicles are needed as the competition in the sport increases. Still, much of the friendly competition that existed out on the trail remains in the sport.

"Generally, all of the competitors are good buddies, both during and outside of the competition," explains Mello. "If a rig breaks down, competitors will often offer parts or assistance to get the broken machine moving again. We all want to win but not by default. This trend is true across most motor sports. No matter how large rockcrawling becomes, it will never be just about the business."[16]

Some competitors were good enough buddies to link up and form official teams. One such organization is Rock Runner Racing, owned and managed by George Wadeson. Based in Rapid City, South Dakota, Rock Runner Racing consists of Tracy Jordan, Don Robbins, Jason Paule, Travis Wadeson, and George Wadeson. For the last few years, the team has used four vehicles that were built at Twisted Customs, the shop owned by one of the drivers, Jason Paule.

According to George Wadeson, the team has been competing since 1999. "At that time," says Wadeson, "a fellow named Bob Hazel was organizing 4WD events and helped start competitive rockcrawling. We participated in Bob's first event, the Warn **Winch** Challenge, in '99. Another promoter, Ranch Pratt, began selling the American Rockcrawling Association (ARCA) as another competitive venue. Back then, we participated in all of Bob Hazel's events and all of the ARCA competitions."[17]

"Each year, there are 12 to 16 events all over the country. Our team consistently places in the top five. We're not trying to win every event, but our goal is stay in that top five. Last year, Tracy Jordan won the UROC Pro-National Super Modified Championship, and Jason Paule came in third. This year, we'll compete in the CalROCS and the UROC series. We won't be doing Bob Hazel's events this year."[18]

Jeff Mello steers his vehicle up the last few yards towards the peak of a hill. A dramatic drop awaits him on the other side, and the new challenge of finding the best way to maneuver down.

"The next few years will test the sport, and we'll see if it's growing like people think it is. If these events can draw 10,000 to 15,000 people each, then media coverage and sponsorship will take off. But, the sport is still going through some growing pains and is probably five years away from being what I envision it to be. That is, real sponsorship behind 20 to 30 drivers of professional status. Those sponsors will keep supporting the drivers, whether they finish first or finish last."[19]

"Sponsorship will also pave the way for new technology to enter the sport. The capital provided by larger companies will allow major advances. Imagine hydrogen-powered rock crawlers, or electric motors spinning each wheel individually.

We're excited about the technological future, but as a team we try not to get caught up in the latest trend. When rear-wheel steering appeared, all of sudden everyone had to have it. We try to be consistent and stick with what we know and what works. Remember, driving experience accounts for about 95 percent of success. But I've been doing some work with Toyota, and there's definitely some exciting stuff out there."[20]

Tracy Jordan, 28 years old and last year's champ in the UROC Super Modified class, sets high goals. "I always try for a podium finish. You have to average third if you want to win the season championship. And, as competition increases, you might even have to do better than that."[21] Though Jordan knows the value of winning a championship, his competitive roots don't stretch as deep as, say, those of Walker Evans. "I started by trail riding on the weekends," recalls Jordan. "I bought a Toyota Land Cruiser for hunting but started hanging out with the 'wrong' people and was soon interested in the challenges of crawling. After only three months of trail riding, I entered my first competition, an ARCA event."[22] But success didn't come instantly for Jordan, as he placed close to dead last in his first event. "It didn't matter, though, because I had gotten the bug."[23]

Another member of Rock Runner Racing, Jason Paule, now 30, has had that "bug"[24] since an early age. "I've been four-wheeling ever since I was born. In fact, I was 6 days old when my parents took me out on the trail for the first time. They were always involved in four-wheeling. My dad also did some off-road racing in the late '60s and early '70s. I was raised in a farm environment, and everyone used 4WD in the winter. There was a natural progression into rockcrawling. In my first event, which was ARCA's second event ever, I placed in the top 20 of about 60 competitors."[25]

Paule has the special responsibility of building the rigs for the team. Creation is part of his background, as his former occupation suggests. "I worked as a professional airbrush artist for a casino," explains Paule. "I was doing the rockcrawling on the side. Eventually, that job would have taken me to Las Vegas, so I started my shop, Twisted Customs, here in South Dakota. We build some pretty radical vehicles here, but we also do lower key modifications. If someone buys a stock Jeep and wants a roll cage built, we'll do that. But we'll also fabricate a chassis from the ground up."[26]

According to Paule, Rock Runner Racing was somewhat groundbreaking, in that it was one of the first teams to compete. "At first it was kind of a joke, teaming up, but now it's more of a mainstay," says Paule.[27] But despite the team spirit, Paule recognizes that his largest competition comes from within. "When we're out competing, Tracy Jordan is my biggest competition," he says. "But we still work as a team, trying to figure out a game plan."[28] Paule echoes the same feelings as Jeff Mello, explaining that despite the intense competition, teams will always help one another. "If someone else breaks, you help. You can't beat someone if they're not running."[29]

Men are not the only ones in this sport. Take Kelli Clifford of South Lake, California. In 2003, she won a title in the Women's Rockcrawling Championship at Cedar City, Utah, in the Unlimited Class. "I've been competing professionally for about three years now," says Clifford. "I started back in 2001, at CalROCS. But I've been wheeling on and off for 19 years, and I started to get a lot more extreme about eight years ago. I'm addicted to the sport, probably even more than a lot of the guys."[30]

Julie Mello smiles from within the framework of roll bars that are designed to protect the driver. Mello has proven her superior driving skill and courage in many rockcrawling competitions.

Like many of the guys, Kelli sees trail riding as the beginning of the sport. But the transition to competition happened with haste. "This pastime quickly evolved into a professional sport,"[31] she explains. Unlike some of her male counterparts, Kelli Clifford has a different take on the sport's camaraderie. "Some people used to be more competitive, but I think they realized the saying, 'what goes around comes around.' That is, helping someone else can help you in the future. I think women in the sport have especially helped some of the men loosen up and be friendlier to their competitors."[32]

To Kelli, the sport is more than just competing in season. During the off-season, she finds that she misses the other drivers. "I just can't wait to see them when competition starts up again."[33] Her love for the sport shines through regardless of the circumstances during the competition. "No matter how difficult the course, you'll always see me with a smile on my face,"[34] she triumphs.

Drivers like Walker Evans, Jeff Mello, Tracy Jordan, Jason Paule, and Kelli Clifford have found success in the sport of rockcrawling. Some of their good fortune is due to their superior driving abilities and courage in hairy situations. But another part of their success depends on the difficult task performed by their **spotters**. Though the drivers might get all the glory, the spotters direct the vehicles down the winning path.

Few know spotting as well as Lance Clifford. He is the husband of Kelli Clifford and a former driver himself. Lance spots for Mike Schaffer, and in 2002, they won a championship together. It takes a special edge and a good measure of humility to be a successful spotter. "Spotting involves a lot more manual labor, such as pulling ropes, stacking boulders. It's labor intensive," says Clifford. "At the end of the event, the driver is clean and ready to go out on the town, while the spotter is filthy and ready for bed."[35] But spotting is not only about brute strength. In fact, the mental challenge is what attracted Lance. "It takes a lot of mental capacity in order to keep the vehicle straight,"[36] he explains.

Clifford, a website builder and creator of www.pirate4x4. com, met his teammate when Schaffer was shopping for a website developer. Schaffer mentioned he was looking for a spotter, and Clifford remarked, "I'll do it."[37] They won the first event in which they competed together. "Chemistry and

communication are the keys to good spotter/driver relation-
ships. There's a lot of turnover because it's hard for a driver
to find someone who will get in front of a 300-horse power.
vehicle and pull it."[38] Jeff Mello's experience is a case study.
"I've used 16 different spotters so far," he says. "It takes the
perfect person."[39]

For one of the most comprehensive overviews of rockcrawling on the Internet, be sure to visit Lance Clifford's
website, *www.pirate4x4.com*. In 1996, Lance started www.
pirate4x4.com as a club site, but just like the sport of rockcrawling, it grew into something much larger and more
professional. As of 2005, www.pirate4x4.com is the sport's
largest website, serving 24 million pages to one million
unique viewers every month. Additionally, there are 40,000

Rockcrawling teams typi-
cally have two competi-
tors, along with a ground
crew and supporters. The driver heads things up from
behind the wheel. The second team member, a "spotter,"
helps to scope out the landscape and provide direc-
tive information about the course and its upcoming
obstacles. Teams race against time and a landscape
that combines off-road driving with unique navigational
challenges.

Over 65 crawlers competed in the Super Modified class
of the 2004 UROC SuperCrawl III, in Salt Lake City, Utah.
Another 35 took part in the Modified class competition.

Julie Mello displays skillful driving as she maintains a precarious balance on three wheels while running over a boulder.

registered members, which continues to increase. The site includes product reviews, chats, live coverage of events, updates, scores, trail reports, and a section devoted to lost and stolen rigs. But where the website shines in its images of rockcrawling. The pictures provide a technical and competitive glimpse into the sport and reveal how much fun is being had out on the trails.

3

WHAT IS IT? THE ROCKS AND THE RIGS

Still relatively new to the world of automotive competition, rockcrawling was made "official" in 1999. Now, this little-known adrenaline-filled activity has turned into a full-blown automotive athletic event, and it regularly draws thousands of people.

This extreme sport combines innovative engineering and driving techniques, with teams typically made up of two competitors—the driver and the spotter—along with a ground crew and supporters. Spotters often use a tow strap to assist in tugging a vehicle over a ridge or to help weight a vehicle that is about to roll.

Though crowds like carnage—and there can be plenty of vehicle-mangling rollovers—they also reward the best drivers, the best rigs, and the best effort to achieve success over the gnarly and tough obstacles.

One of the most exciting original courses was in Farmington, New Mexico. It was designed by resident Phillip Collard for what was reportedly the 70 best rockcrawlers in the world, who showed up for a two-day event, in September 1999. Collard, a staff member of ARCA at that time, was

Jeff Mello is shown acting as spotter for driver Julie Mello during a rockcrawling competition. The spotter uses a tow strap to pull and guide the vehicle over the ridge.

involved in building all nine courses of the ARCA events during the next season. He built 14-obstacle "puzzles" with flags or gates. Drivers and spotters had to figure out the lines and have the courage to go for it since many of the obstacles defied the laws of gravity. The courses were designed for the safety of spectators and set up in a **Tread Lightly!** environmentally friendly fashion.

Things have changed dramatically from the first year of the ARCA series in 1999, when drivers put their foot to the floor and throttled their rigs up and over boulders and rock ledges. It quickly became a professional sport, with extensive modifications to the rigs. As a result, the series has drawn more sponsors, originally led by Goodyear Tire & Rubber Company and Skyjacker Suspensions, along with other well-known names in the off-road business such as Currie Enterprises, Detroit Lockers, and Warn Winch. Today, Goodyear has been replaced by BFGoodrich as a primary sponsor of the sport. This tire company has put a huge emphasis on developing rockcrawling tires and has used many of the top competitors as guides to help out with the best and newest designs.

The list of sponsors today, is evidence of how popular rockcrawling has become. For, 2005, UROC sponsors include Skyjacker Suspensions, Toyo Tires, FabTech Suspensions, BFGoodrich, Rough Country Suspension, Goodyear Tire & Rubber Company, Tuff Country Suspensions, Maxxis Tires, TerraFlex, Warn Winch, Advance Adapters, Aero Turbine Exhaust, Rhino Off-Road, Four Wheel Parts, ProComp Tires, Power Tank, American Racing, BullyDog Diesel Tech, KC HiLites, and Moser Engine. The UROC works with Jeep and Toyota as well.

The list of sponsors shows that the main feature of rockcrawling is the vehicles. These big-tired trucks and **moon buggies** are outfitted with flexible suspensions (so their tires and wheels can stretch to keep contact with the rocks) and have been modified to crawl across the uneven landscape of rocks, boulders, and mountainsides that are found most often in the American West. While vehicles are searching for their footing across the terrain, spectators perch on outcroppings and flat rock faces to get the best views of their favorite teams.

In addition to outdoor or natural courses, one of the latest developments in rockcrawling is manmade rock courses.

The ever-popular Jeep has been used for decades to travel through woodland terrain. Now, Jeep, BF Goodrich, and other automotive manufacturers have helped popularize the sport of rockcrawling by sponsoring rockcrawling events.

Tom Collins is a well-known and respected off-road expert. Collins spends more than 100 days out of each year in the business of four-wheeling. He is a product specialist, working for Land Rover (as well as other manufacturers and training 4WD instructors) and building off-road courses. In 2004, Collins built a highly regarded rockcrawling course, in Indianapolis, Indiana. It was built of manmade materials.

"Indoor courses (or manmade courses) will alleviate some of the concerns associated with rockcrawling. They're a must for the sport to move forward. There's always compromise involved,"[40] explained George Wadeson, owner of Rock Runner Racing. "When I started trail riding, part of it was because I loved the outdoors and the ability to get away. Now, the sport may be finding itself in large metropolitan areas because it needs to draw from a large fan base. When we built our trailers to tow the vehicles, we left them open so we could maneuver them into tricky terrain. The irony is that these trailers could easily be sitting in flat parking lots while we're climbing terrain. We could have gone with a closed trailer."[41]

"We are currently building manmade courses in Phoenix, Arizona, Portland, Indiana, and Las Vegas, Nevada. We chose these sites as a result of geographic location (they are spread around the country), the area's population, and the demographics of the people in theses areas,"[42] says Ranch Pratt. Pratt built the first course of synthetic materials in the country for the Specialty Equipment Manufacturer's Association (SEMA) show in the fall of 2004, in Las Vegas.

"On manmade courses, we generally have eight obstacles. Each team is given ten minutes to get through the course. They are somewhat steeper than natural obstacles (up to 75 degrees.) and between 10 to 25 feet tall. We also build technical obstacles, which are not tall but have steep, short crevasses and deep holes. These types of obstacles allow us to lay out cones in such a way that they become technical to drive. The end goal of a manmade or natural course is a combination of steep, tall point-and-shoot obstacles and twisted, technical-thinking obstacles."[43]

A course in Salt Lake City, is 600 by 200 feet, with eight obstacles that was constructed in a month. It is made from construction refuse and dirt and is covered with four to 10

Brian Howard drops off a cliff that he just climbed called *Full Throttle*, one of ten obstacles on a wooded rockcrawling course in Jellico, Tennessee. Extreme vehicles like Howard's are in the Super Modified class and can have tires up to 40 inches high, rear steering, any motor configuration, and any shape chassis. A single seat is OK, and no body panels are required.

inches of concrete that is pumped and sprayed on by a hose. The fiber in the concrete makes it stronger.

While television and other media outlets have covered rockcrawling for a number of years, its popularity has brought even more coverage. And, having the manmade courses helps the television crews, who don't have to lug their equipment up and over the rocks in the middle of the back country to get good footage. Television and media coverage for 2004 included *ESPN*, *CBS Evening News*, *Inside Edition*, *Discovery Channel*, *Spike*, *OLN*, *Newsweek*, *The New York Times*, along with all 4WD magazines and 4x4 Internet publications. "For 2005, *ESPN* will be doubling its coverage to 90 million households. *OLN* will be airing our events 39 times, or reaching 30 million households."[43]

The Rigs

The vehicles have changed, too. Before the sport was official and people were just trail riding, a typical vehicle might have been a Jeep Wrangler with 33-inch tires and jacked up suspension. Some may have included roll cages, for safety. As the competition increased, however, drivers and enthusiasts began investing more time and money into their rigs to get better performance. As a result, sanctioning bodies such as UROC decided to classify vehicles, so one team would not automatically win because its vehicle was more sophisticated than the others.

Some drivers prefer to compete in vehicles similar to publicly available models. For example, Jeff Mello, who runs in the Stock Modified class, has driven a street-legal 1979 Jeep Wrangler CJ-7 with larger tires in the past. This truck features an AMC 360-horsepower V8 engine, T-18 transmission, Dana 44 front and Detroit Locker rear axles, a Detroit 300 transfer case, 4.56 gears, Skyjacker Softride springs, and 35-inch BFGoodrich Krawler tires on 15x10-inch Centerline wheels. Mello's engine uses an Edelbrock intake and a direct-injection propane fuel system. He's working on a modified Jeep, but it will still resemble a vehicle you would see at a dealership.

Other rockcrawling rigs are more radical in design though they keep the look of a model that could have come from a factory. For the 2004 season, Tracy Jordan drove a vehicle he called *The Matrix* because the headlights, hood, and fenders came from a Toyota Matrix. Jordan and his team, Rock Runner Racing, got the Toyota parts right off

Vehicles in the Stock Modified class, like Jeff Mello's Jeep CJ-7 pictured here, are street legal, have 35-inch tires, a full body, and must meet safety requirements.

the assembly line before Toyota's Matrix even debuted to the public. But his rig is far from a standard Toyota Matrix. The entire chassis and frame were built by hand at Twisted Customs, the shop owned by Jordan's teammate, Jason Paule. *The Matrix* is powered by a V6 engine attached to a turbocharged 350 transmission, and it has special and more aggressive Dana 60 axles. The engine is up front as it would be in a normal vehicle.

As Jordan explains, at first it was important for the rock-crawling rigs to resemble factory-built vehicles because the sponsors wanted to attach their names to more recognizable products. So, some rigs had "**skins**"[45] along the sides to make them look stock. "But once we started winning," explains Jordan, "that changed. Our main sponsor now, FabTech (Suspensions), doesn't care what the rig looks like, just as long as its sticker is on the winning one."[46]

Rigs are constantly evolving. Back in 2003, Walker Evans had a Chevy S-10-based rockcrawler that was revolutionary. Though Evans' truck ran on 40-inch Goodyear MT/Rs, also known as Rock Spiders, the radical part was the suspension. This vehicle, completely hand-built, used fully independent suspension (this means each wheel has its own suspension set-up). Before this, many competitors were concerned that fully independent suspensions would never hold up. Remember, this is a tough sport on vehicles, so the durability of solid axles was usually appreciated. With solid axles, the suspension system works both wheels along the front or rear axle. Using tricky engineering, Evans created with a setup that did not compromise ground clearance or cause excess tire rubbing, which can sometimes happen with this type of setup. His team developed CV halfshafts (this is the support system in the middle of the axle) that were larger than those used in GM's one-ton trucks and in the Hummer H1 to maintain strength.

Today, many rigs don't look anything like factory-built vehicles. Competitors in the Super Modified and Unlimited classes drive built-for-the-extreme vehicles, sometimes called moon buggies. The advantage of these buggies is that they don't have to resemble everyday trucks. For example, Lance Clifford's vehicle, which is driven by Mike Schaffer, is a hand-built moon buggy that uses a four-cylinder Subaru boxer engine putting out 350 horsepower. The engine sits

Jason Scherer is shown driving *Tiny*, a rig in the Super Modified class, and first of the mid-engine, single seat style of vehicle now commonly referred to as a moon buggy.

in the mid-rear, all four wheels steer, and there is just one seat. Lance's wife, Kelli, competes in a single-seat buggy and recognizes its playful nature. "I kind of think of it as a go-cart,"[46] she says.

These lunar-like vehicles are beginning to take the sport over. Drivers not using them often envy them. For example, Tracy Jordan, who won the UROC Super Modified championship last year in *The Matrix*, is ready to make the transition. "Personally," says Jordan, "I don't want to compete in that truck another year. I'd like to go buggy. I figure, if you're gonna spend 50 grand every few years on a vehicle, you want to be state-of-the-art in order to be competitive."[48]

The popularity of rockcrawling has captured the attention of some of the auto manufacturers in the United States, too. At the 2005 North American International Auto Show in Detroit, Michigan, held in January of 2005, DaimlerChrysler showed a radical new concept vehicle called the Jeep Hurricane. With two 5.7-liter Hemi V8 engines, the Hurricane has a combined 670 horsepower and 740 lb./ft. of torque. But the real innovation is in the steering. All four wheels can be pointed inward, and when one side spins one way and the other side spins the opposite way, the Hurricane can rotate on its axis or center. The wheels will also turn 90 degrees in the same direction, allowing this moon buggy-like vehicle to be driven sideways in a kind of crab-like motion. When making a normal turn, the back wheels will turn slightly to reduce the turning circle. While the Hurricane may never make it to production, some of its elements, including the innovative steering, may be included in future Jeep products that you or your family might drive.

Many rockcrawlers, though, have had these notions in their heads for years. "There are no new ideas in this sport," says Jeff Mello. "It just takes someone with some capital (money) to invest in the ideas and make them into viable realities."[49] Now that rockcrawling has grown, it's beginning to influence decisions made by the car companies. Back in the trail riding days, people were taking stock Jeeps and Land Rovers and modifying them for off-road use. That was all they had. Now, the auto manufacturers are responding to the sport's popularity by spending millions of dollars in developing advanced off-road machines for everyday use, for fun, or for competition.

The Tires

As is the case of all motorsports, tires are one of the most critical components on a vehicle. They're the part that contacts the surface, therefore must function well. Jeff Mello puts it nicely: "The tire is the part that you both blame the most and champion or recognize the most."[50] A lot of competitors today are running BFGoodrich Krawler™ tires. Tracy Jordan estimates that about four out of five drivers rely on them today. In fact, Jordan was approached by BFGoodrich when they were developing the tire. "I worked for about a year on the tire, trying to find the perfect tread pattern," says Jordan. "In 2002, nobody was on Krawlers™, and now probably 80 percent of the rockcrawling competitors use them."[51]   Jeff

DID YOU KNOW?

While people can go rockcrawling almost anywhere they find rocks, most rockcrawling competitions take place in the Southwest, including New Mexico and Utah, and California. A favorite spot for many events is just outside of Farmington, New Mexico. The landscape in this region is perfectly suited to rockcrawling. Nestled in the picturesque San Juan River Valley, within sight of Colorado's rugged San Juan Mountains and the desert highlands of Arizona and Utah, outdoor enthusiasts know Farmington well as a major destination for rock climbing, camping, and hiking. This area has been a tourist destination for decades and a rockcrawler's dream location for years.

Jeeps are not the only vehicles on which competitors base Stock Modified vehicles. In fact, a popular small SUV in the rockcrawling world is the Suzuki Samurai.

Tires are one of the most critical components of a vehicle. The tread on these BF Goodrich Krawlers™ enable the vehicles shown here to grip the rock walls and squeeze though a narrow pass.

Mello was approached by BFGoodrich for advice when the Krawler™ was under development.

BFGoodrich offers two Krawler™ tires: one that is fully treaded and one that is half treaded and blank (or slick) on the other side. Many rockcrawlers use the fully treaded model but cut the tire to their own specification. This may include gouging out sections of rubber compound or slicing large knobs to increase the surface area and grip. At the moment, BFGoodrich is developing another new and improved Krawler™. "But I don't know how they could improve that tire anymore," says Jordan. "It's just so good."[52]

Though BFGoodrich is today's king, other tire manufacturers are involved in developing rockcrawling tires and supporting the competitors. Long-time racer Walker Evans swears by his Rock Spiders. Another tire brand, Toyo, is testing its luck in the sport. Lance Clifford's team recently picked up Toyo as a sponsor, and he's eager to give them a try. "Right now," says Clifford, "there are no top people running Toyos since everything is dominated by BFGoodrich. So we'll see how they do."[53]

4

THE RULES AND DEFINITIONS

Rockcrawling has three series in the United States: The Sportsman Invitational events are put on by rockcrawling organizations around the country and are sanctioned by UROC. Neuroc is a fantastic example of this (*www.neuroc. com*). Hundreds of teams from around the country compete in their local area under the UROC banner.

The Extreme Nationals series is split into Eastern and Western divisions with three events in each division's series. Generally, 60 teams compete per event. This is the semi-pro series. If a team does well in the Sportsman Invitational series, it moves up to the Extreme Nationals. Crowds here are big, ranging from 6,000 to 10,000 per two-day event. Even bigger crowds are expected in 2005, with manmade courses now set up in metropolitan areas.

The ProNationals is the coveted series in which only the best of the best compete. It is nationwide with five regular season events. There are a maximum of 60 teams, with between 10,000 to 20,000 spectators, with larger audiences expected in 2005.

As with any organized and competitive sport, there are rules and regulations for those who participate in the events. There are rules for the owner/driver and spotter, specifications for the vehicle, and regulations for how the competition takes place and how it is scored.

Let's take a look at some of the 2005 rules from UROC. We'll start with UROC's purpose and goals: UROC's primary interests are to enhance safety for spectators and participants, as well as to promote rockcrawling as a major motor sport. Rules and regulations are the minimum acceptable standards for competition and are intended as a guide for the conduct of the sport.

The primary responsibility for the safe conditions and operation during a rockcrawling competition is with the vehicle's owner, driver, and spotter. Each competitor must agree, that at all times while riding in a vehicle and participating in an event, to wear approved seat and shoulder belts and helmet correctly. The owner/driver promises that he/she/they have inspected their vehicle, it is in good mechanical condition, and it meets all rules.

UROC has four categories of vehicles: Super-Modified, Modified, Stock and Exhibition, and the Super-Modified class is for the most bold and daring 4WD vehicles in use today. The Modified class is for vehicles that the general population can relate to (those that look like a vehicle your family might drive or you could buy at a dealership) but still have enough freedom in design to make modifications (or changes) that make them capable of extreme performance in rockcrawling.

The Stock class is for those who want to use 4WD vehicles with readily available, bolt-on aftermarket parts. (These are parts that you can buy through a dealer or automotive shop.) Restrictions say these must be two-seat, front engine,

This vehicle is in the Modified, or Legends, class. Modifieds have two seats, the motor in front, front axle steering, recognizable body panels, and tires up to a maximum of 37 inches high.

full-frame, and full-body vehicles. The Exhibition class is for any vehicle that does not meet the restrictions for the other classes and are for exhibition only. They are not formally included in the event and cannot collect series points, purses, or trophies.

Competitors are the driver, spotter and/or alternate spotter signed up to compete in an event. The driver is the person on the team who controls the vehicle while riding in it, and the spotter is the person on the team who directs the driver from outside of the vehicle. The team is considered the driver, spotter, alternate spotter, owner, and all support personnel.

Custom, or custom-made, refers to items for the vehicle or competition which are produced for specific applications in limited quantities. Original Equipment Manufacturer (OEM) means the same parts or items that you would install on a vehicle from the factory. Readily available items are mass produced by commercial means and available for purchase through any conventional distribution channel including the Internet, catalogs, stores, manufacturer sales program, and shops.

UROC has Vehicle Specifications and Definitions. Let's take a look at a few: Axles are the link between the wheels on front and rear ends. They begin at the end of the drive shaft (this is the unit that transmits power from the engine and transmission to the axels and it then goes to the wheels) and end at the flange for wheels but do not include brake assemblies. All axle widths, live axles, solid axles, independent, and military-style drop-in axles are permitted.

Gear reduction may be prior to the axles, after the axles or a combination of both.

Manual wheelbase changes are allowed during an event though the wheelbase may not be manually changed while competing on an obstacle.

Differentials must have some form of 100 percent locking ability, which means the wheels along one axle, or both, are locked together and rotating at the same speed. Vent tubes must be attached to a fluid containment container. Vehicles are limited to two axles, which must be of an automotive type and duty as determined by an UROC Official Inspector. There are additional restrictions for Modified and for Stock vehicles.

The body is the outer layer of the vehicle and includes the floor, sides, rear, hood, fender, grill, and firewall. Body

An off-roader checks underneath his vehicle. Drivers, spotters, and vehicle owners are responsible for the safe condition and operation of their vehicles while participating in rockcrawling events.

panels may be made of steel, aluminum, fiberglass, polycarbonate (Lexan), carbon fiber, or plastic. If used, front inner fenders must have a 3-inch hole that is used for fire suppression access. Additional restrictions for Modified vehicles require that they must have two front outer fenders that closely match the original factory configuration; vehicles not from the factory must obtain approval from a tech marshal prior to the event. In the Stock class, vehicles must be from the factory and a four-wheel drive product, with outer and inner front fenders mounted to the main portion of the passenger compartment, or cowl, and must extend to the grille. This includes the outer and inner fender unless otherwise constructed by OEM manufacturer. All OEM fenders are approved for competition.

There are no restrictions for the grille for the Super-Modified class, but the grilles of Modified vehicles must closely match the original factory configuration of an OEM vehicle and work in this configuration with the hood, fenders, and tub/cab. Grilles must include two headlights in the stock location (if applicable). Light stickers or off-road driving lights mounted in the original location of the headlights may be used as a substitute. Stock grilles must be an OEM configuration, of a size approved by UROC officials, and have the same headlight restrictions.

The hood must be designed to protect the occupants and cover the top of the engine completely, including the heads, manifold, valve covers, block, alternator, water pump, fan, radiator, and fuel injection system no matter where the engine is located. Scoops and breather holes are acceptable, but those larger than 14 square inches must be screened and the sum dimension of all breather holes may not exceed 20 percent of total hood area. A hood may be substituted by an occupant shield, which must separate the driver from the engine completely when used in conjunction with the firewall and may be made from 3/16-inch fire retardant Lexan. Additional restrictions for Modified and Stock vehicles exist, again matching to their OEM or factory configuration.

The tub/cab (the main compartment for the driver/spotter) must be in good shape with firewalls that meet specific requirements for fire safety and are completely separate the occupants from the engine compartment. All vehicles must have a floor under and between the driver and passenger seat for the occupants to rest their feet and to protect them from flying parts during breakage. Additional restrictions apply to Modified and Stock vehicles: Brakes are defined by UROC as the source of control for slowing and stopping wheels. Mechanically operated and hydraulic-assisted brakes are permitted.

Bumpers consist of the front bumper to connect the foremost part of the frame excluding push bars, stingers, etc. The rear bumper connects the rearmost part of the frame and the rearmost part of the vehicle. Bumpers must connect the right and left frame rails.

UROC considers the following to be part of the cooling system: radiators, hoses, engine ports, heater hoses, and coolant product. Air cooling and water-cooled systems are permitted. The radiator must be covered so, in the event of a break in the radiator, spectators, spotters, and drivers are protected from the coolant spill.

Drive shafts are the working link between the transfer case and the axles. Mechanical drive shafts are required and must be covered so they may not be touched from the passenger compartment. There must be complete shielding between the occupant(s) and any drive shaft u-joint. Drive shafts that could fail and swing to hit occupant(s) must be caged for protection.

Electrical components includes all wires, lights, batteries, and any other item controlled by or conducting electricity as its function. Batteries must be the non-pill type and in good shape with adequate mounting to keep the battery in place in the event of a roll. Mounting must be a clamp type mount that cages the battery in position. Foot-type clamp mounting is not approved. Wires must be in a safe condition

A man performs maintenance on the drive shaft of his vehicle. The drive shaft must be covered so that it cannot come into contact with the occupants of the vehicle, and it must meet various other safety requirements.

and position. Exposed or burnt wires are not approved. A master kill switch that shuts down at least the fuel pump (if electrical) and ignition system is required.

The engine is the system designed to create torque and horsepower. The engine must be free of fluid leaks that pose a fire threat, and vent tubes must be attached to a fluid containment container of an appropriate type. The engine must be of an automotive type, design, and duty as determined by UROC officials prior to the event. For Modified vehicles, the majority of the engine must be in front of the foot pedals. For Stock, the entire engine must be in front of the foot pedals.

The frame of a vehicle is the two rails supporting the mounting of the body and drive train as the main frame, and connecting cross members as the sub frame. Any OEM or custom-built frame is permitted. OEM unibody construction is permitted. All frame material must be magnetic steel. Other restrictions apply for Modified and Stock.

The fuel system includes all components and connections used to store, deliver, and mix fuel and air on the vehicle. This includes the type of fuel used. Carburetors are permitted. Fuel injection systems that inject fuel from a throttle body or through ports are permitted. Non-vented gas caps are permitted. Unleaded, leaded, propane, natural gas, and diesel fuels are permitted. Nitromethane or alcohol-based fuels are not allowed. Nitrous oxide is allowed. (Hand throttles are approved, with some restrictions.)

Roll bars or roll cages are the safety bars surrounding the occupants. Designed to protect the occupants in the vent of a rollover. A six-point mounting cage that protects all seats in a vehicle is required and must be constructed of material meeting or exceeding required minimums.

Roll cage padding is required on all roll cage bars that may come in contact with the driver's or spotter's head. Any high-back production seat for full-sized adults is permitted that is designed for automotive use. The seat must have a five-point harness (lap, two shoulder, and submarine), and the harness must be worn at all times while competing. Seats must be mounted to the roll cage. Seat configuration must incorporate whiplash protection, and the head rest must be at proper height for the driver. When properly

A group of spectators watch Jeff Mello descend a rock fall. The roll bars are another safety feature that protects the driver in the event of a rollover.

strapped in, the driver should not be able to lean out the side of the cage.

UROC considers steering to be all components designed to turn the vehicle's wheels to the left or right of the vehicle centerline. Full hydraulic steering and brake steering is permitted.

Suspension pivot points, connecting points, etc., must be free of cracks and in good physical condition as determined by an UROC official. Reactive suspension systems are permitted. Manually controlled suspension systems are

approved but may not control individual tires. These systems must control the entire front axle and/or the entire
rear axle.

Winches may be used to control axle movement but not
individual tires. Any types of pneumatic construction, bias,
bias belted and radial tires are permitted. Individual lugs
may be cut but not fully removed. No more than 50 percent of each lug may be removed. Tire size is limited to 48
inches in diameter, measured using a measuring device and
measuring the diameter on the wheels that will be used for
competition with the vehicle on the ground measuring in a
horizontal plane at the tire center line with 12 pounds per

BFGoodrich offers two
versions of its popular
Krawler tire. One is fully
treaded, and the other features a "blank" tread area on
half the tire. Competitors can carve out that blank section to create a pattern that best fits their needs.

Though rockcrawling is still small compared to other
off-road automotive events, it is growing quickly. Its
unique appeal comes from its physical challenges, combined with an up-close and personal view of natural sur-
roundings. As with all off-road driving, this carries with
it a certain responsibility: participants and fans must
have a balance between enjoying the sport they love
and respecting the land on which that sport depends.
Remember to tread lightly!

Drivers are required to wear helmets and have more than a little courage.

square inch (psi) of air pressure. (This value may be adjusted for regional competition.) Tires are to be the only source of forward, side, or back movement of the vehicle. Tires must be inflated with air, nitrogen, carbon dioxide (CO_2), commercial weight enhancing products, or water. Vehicles must have four independent tires. The maximum tire diameter for Super-modified is 37 inches, measured with a measuring device. Modifieds are restricted to a maximum tire diameter of 35 inches, measured with a measuring device. Tires must be DOT (Department of Transportation) approved.

The transfer case transfers power to the front axle and rear axle of a vehicle. Only mechanical transfer cases (manually or automatically operated) are permitted.

The following wheels are approved for competition: all steel and aluminum wheels. Bead locks are recommended. However, wheels and bead locks must not interfere with the proper operation of brakes.

Weight is the total vehicle weight not including driver, spotter, or any equipment not normally carried while competing. It does include normal vehicle fluids. The vehicle must weigh at least 2,500 pounds and weight reduction based on damage while competing may be approved by a UROC marshal.

Professionally built and sold electric, hydraulic, and power take–off winches, with a single line pull rating of at least 5,000 pounds are required. Clevis hooks must be rated at 10,000 pounds. Vehicles must carry an approved winch weight bag, which can be carried in a bag by the competitor and left at the start gate of each obstacle.

A minimum of two fire extinguishers must be mounted in the vehicle and must be easily accessible.

The vehicle must contain a basic first aid kit. It can be carried in a bag by the competitor and left at the start gate of each obstacle.

Driver helmets must meet specifications. Spotters are required to wear their helmet at all times, as well.

Penalty points and/or disqualification can be issued for infractions to UROC rules.

NOTES

Chapter 1

1   Sue Mead's interview with Ranch Pratt, January 2005.

2   Ibid.

3   Ibid.

4   Ibid.

5   Ibid.

6   Ibid.

7   Ibid.

8   Ibid.

Chapter 2

9   Sue Mead's interview with Walker Evans, February 16, 2005.

10   Ibid.

11   Ibid.

12   Ibid.

13   Ibid.

14   Sue Mead's interview with Jeff Mello, January 25, 2005.

15   Ibid.

16   Ibid.

17   Sue Mead's interview with George Wadeson, January 25, 2005.

18   Ibid.

19   Ibid.

20   Ibid.

21   Sue Mead's interview with Tracey Jordan, January 26, 2005.

22   Ibid.

23   Ibid.

24   Sue Mead's interview with Jason Paule, January 26, 2005.

25   Ibid.

26   Ibid.

27   Ibid.

28   Ibid.

29   Ibid.

30 Sue Mead's interview with Kelli Clifford, January 27, 2005.

31 Ibid.

32 Ibid.

33 Ibid.

34 Ibid.

35 Sue Mead's interview with Lance Clifford, February 19, 2005.

36 Ibid.

37 Ibid.

38 Ibid.

39 Sue Mead's interview with Jeff Mello.

Chapter 3

40 Sue Mead's interview with George Wadeson.

41 Ibid.

42 Sue Mead's interview with Ranch Pratt.

43 Ibid.

44 Ibid.

45 Sue Mead's interview with Tracy Jordan.

46   Ibid.

47   Sue Mead's interview with Kelli Clifford.

48   Sue Mead's interview with Tracy Jordan.

49   Sue Mead's interview with Jeff Mello.

50   Ibid.

51   Sue Mead's interview with Tracy Jordan.

52   Ibid.

53   Sue Mead's interview with Lance Clifford.

CHRONOLOGY

1999 Ranch Pratt formed the American Rockcrawlers Association (ARCA) and began the first rockcrawling series of competitions.

2000 The American Rockcrawlers Association changes its name to the Rockcrawlers Association of America (RCAA).

2002 Craig Stumph formed the Utah Rockcrawling & Off-Road Challenge.

2003 The United Rockcrawling & Off-Road Challenge was formed (UROC).

2004 The first rockcrawling course made of synthetic materials was built by Ranch Pratt.

STATISTICS

Rockcrawling Events:
>One in 1999
>Four in 2000
>16 in 2005

Rockcrawling Competitors (registered teams):
>49 in 1999
>180 in 2005

Rockcrawling Sportsmen:
>Approximately 400 in the United States

Rockcrawling Events on Manmade Courses:
>None in 1999
>Eight scheduled in 2005

GLOSSARY

American Rockcrawlers Association (ARCA) The organization was the original rockcrawling organization, created by Ranch Pratt, along with others, that put on their first event in Farmington, New Mexico, in 1999. In 2001 ARCA became the Rockcrawlers Association of America (RCAA).

Moab The Moab region is in Utah on the Colorado Plateau known to four-wheelers and rockcrawlers as some of the best off-road terrain in the country. Trails and rock climbs challenge beginner to expert drivers.

Moon buggy This term refers to a custom-built rig that may include features such as rear-wheel steering, rear-engine placement, and single-position seating. Some of these vehicles look like the Rover vehicle that went to the moon.

Rig This is any specially modified or equipped vehicle to handle off-road or indoor rockcrawling.

Skins This describes the fabricated outside of a vehicle.

Spotter Paired with the driver, the spotter is the person who stays outside the vehicle to help choose the best path over each obstacle during a rockcrawling competition. Often, the job requires manual labor, such as pulling on ropes and sometimes stacking boulders to help assist the vehicle in getting the correct line. It also involves the mental task of making decisions that keep the vehicle upright.

Tread Lightly!, Inc. Like Tread Lightly!, the organization which emphasizes leaving "no trace" with camping, hiking and off-road driving activities, all of the rockcrawling organizations encourage responsible rockcrawling and emphasize their commitment to responsible land use. All groups work to educate rockcrawling teams and fans about the effects of driving off the pavement in these rugged rigs. United Rockcrawling & Off-Road Challange (UROC) emphasizes that the risks of rockcrawling go beyond rolled trucks and other accidents: teams threaten the land whenever they drive across it and must respect it. Likewise, fans must always be aware of where they tread and leave "no trace" from their time watching the competitions.

Technical driving This involves knowing specific driving techniques, such as where to place your tires or how much throttle or brake to use going over an obstacle.

United Rockcrawling & Off-Road Challenge (UROC) UROC is the largest rockcrawling organization and is headed by Mike Patey (President) and Ranch Pratt (CEO).

Winch A machine for hoisting a vehicle into the air. It has wire cables or a rope that winds around a drum as the vehicle is lifted or pulled.

FURTHER READING

Allen, Jim. *Four-Wheeler's Bible*. St. Paul, MN: Motorbooks International, 2002.

Allen, Jim. *Jeep 4x4 Performance Handbook*. St. Paul, MN: Motorbooks International, 1998.

Cole, Nick. *Off-Road Recovery Techniques: A Practical Handbook on the Principles and Use of Equipment*. Croydon, UK: Motor Racing Publications, 1996.

De Long, Brad. *4-Wheel Freedom: The Art of Off-Road Driving*. Boulder, CO: Paladin Press, 1997.

Dimbleby, Nick. *Off-Road Driving Techniques*. Wiltshire, UK: Crowood Press, 1997.

Gorr, Eric. *Motocross & Off Road Performance Handbook* (3rd ed). Osceola, WI: Motorbooks International, 2004.

Hanson, Jonathan, and Roseann Beggy. *Backroad Adventuring in Your Sport Utility Vehicle*. New York, NY: McGraw-Hill, 1998.

Hibbard, Jeff, and Ron Sessions. *Baja Bugs and Buggies*. Tucson, AZ: Berkeley Publishing Group, 1982.

Jackson, Jack. *The Off-Road 4-Wheel Drive Book: Choosing, Using and Maintaining Go-Anywhere Vehicles*. Newbury Park, CA: Haynes Publications, Inc, 1999.

Lewellyn, Harry. *Shifting into 4WD: The SUV Owner's 4WD Handbook*. Costa Mesa, CA: GloveBox Publications, 2003.

Ludel, Moses. *Jeep Owner's Bible*. Cambridge, MA: Bentley Publishers, 1998.

Statham, Steve. *Jeep Color History*. Osceola, WI: Motorbooks International, 1999.

INTERNET SITES

Search terms: rockcrawling; off road; rock crawler.

www.uroc.com

> *The homepage of the United Rockcrawling and Off-Road Challenge, which provides a schedule of events, team and driver profiles, photo and video galleries, and industry news.*

www.calrocs.com

> *The California Rockcrawling and Off-Road Championship Series (CalROCS) includes sponsor information, the official rulebook, a photo gallery, an events schedule, and current news.*

www.pirate4x4.com

> *An enthusiast site developed by Lance Clifford, including discussion forums, chat, legal information, events coverage, trail reports, and even a section for lost/stolen rigs.*

www.walkerevansracing.com

> *The homepage of Walker Evans' racing team, offering products such as wheels, shocks, and fiberglass body panels.*

www.rockrunnerracing.com

> *Rock Runner Racing's homepage includes plenty of pictures, the upcoming schedule, industry news, and biographies of the team members.*

www.off-road.com/rock

> *A monthly site devoted to rockcrawling including a schedule of future events, photo and video galleries, discussion boards, classified ads, and news.*

www.rockcrawler.com

> *Rockcrawler 4x4 and Off-Road Magazine's website featuring message boards, trail reports, technical support, and a merchandise store.*

ADDRESSES

UROC
727 North 1550 East
Second Floor
Orem, UT 84057
(801) 932-0322

Walker Evans Racing
P.O. Box 2469
Riverside, CA 92516
(951) 784-7223

Photo Credits:

INDEX

ABOUT THE AUTHOR

Sue Mead began her automotive career as a part-time freelance evaluator for *Four Wheeler Magazine* in 1988, on the first team that included women as test drivers. Today, she travels the globe test-driving cars and trucks and working as a photojournalist/feature writer for over four dozen publications. Mead specializes in 4WD and has been an auto editor and 4WD editor for CNN/fn. Over the last 18 years, she has accumulated enough off-road miles to have circumnavigated the world in the dirt.

Mead has been a participating journalist on three Camel Trophy adventures in Borneo, Mongolia and Central America. She has been an attending journalist on the following events: the Camel Trophy '98, in Tierra del Fuego, Argentina; for the Land Rover's G4 Challenge, in Australia, in 2003; and for the LONGITUDE team from Singapore to Bangkok, in 2004. She has participated on three record-setting adventure drives: the Arctic Circle Challenge '95, the Tip to Tip Challenge '96, and the TransAmerica Challenge '97. She assisted Mark A. Smith and Jeep Jamboree U.S.A. as the coordinator of the Alaska Jeep Jamborees, in 1996, and 1997.

Mead's off-road racing includes participating in Baja 1000 six times: She was the co-driver for Rod Hall in the 1996 Baja 1000 (1st place finish), was the co-driver for Darren Skilton for the 1999 Baja 1000 (1st place finish), was the co-driver in the Baja 2000 on the internationally ranked Mitsubishi team (1st place finish), was the co-driver on the Scaroni Motorsports Team, 2001, and was the driver for two Wide Open Baja/Centrix Teams in the 2002 and 2003 Baja 1000. She was a driver and co-driver for the Primm 300 (1st place) with Darren Skilton. She was the co-driver in the 2000 Paris–Dakar Rally, completed the Nevada 1000, and is featured in the off-road documentary, *Into the Dust*, as a member of the Toyota Motorsports Team, 2002.

Mead writes for *Four Wheeler*, *Four Wheel & Off Road*, *4WD and Sport Utility*, *Off Road*, *Motor Trend*, *Truck Trend*, *Auto Week*, *Popular Science*, *Popular Mechanics*, *Men's Journal*, *Parade*, *The New York Times*, *Road and Track Buyers Guide*, *European Car*, as well as magazines and newspapers around the globe. She is also a correspondent for Motor Trend Radio and has received two awards from the International Automotive Press Association.

Mead has written *Monster Trucks and Tractors*. New York, NY: Chelsea House Publishers, 1998.

ACKNOWLEDGEMENTS

Special thanks to Robert A. George whose help was instrumental in the research, writing, and editing of this book.

Other thanks to, Ranch Pratt, Walker Evans, Jeff Mello, Tracy Jordan, Jason Paule, Kelli Clifford, and Tom Collins.